AF446686

BUILD BACK BETTER SECTOR GUIDES
VOLUME 2: TRANSPORT

OCTOBER 2024

ASIAN DEVELOPMENT BANK

 Creative Commons Attribution 3.0 IGO license (CC BY 3.0 IGO)

© 2024 Asian Development Bank
6 ADB Avenue, Mandaluyong City, 1550 Metro Manila, Philippines
Tel +63 2 8632 4444; Fax +63 2 8636 2444
www.adb.org

Some rights reserved. Published in 2024.

ISBN 978-92-9270-940-2 (print); 978-92-9270-941-9 (PDF); 978-92-9270-942-6 (ebook)
Publication Stock No. TIM240436-2
DOI: http://dx.doi.org/10.22617/TIM240436-2

The views expressed in this publication are those of the authors and do not necessarily reflect the views and policies of the Asian Development Bank (ADB) or its Board of Governors or the governments they represent.

ADB does not guarantee the accuracy of the data included in this publication and accepts no responsibility for any consequence of their use. The mention of specific companies or products of manufacturers does not imply that they are endorsed or recommended by ADB in preference to others of a similar nature that are not mentioned.

By making any designation of or reference to a particular territory or geographic area in this document, ADB does not intend to make any judgments as to the legal or other status of any territory or area.

This publication is available under the Creative Commons Attribution 3.0 IGO license (CC BY 3.0 IGO) https://creativecommons.org/licenses/by/3.0/igo/. By using the content of this publication, you agree to be bound by the terms of this license. For attribution, translations, adaptations, and permissions, please read the provisions and terms of use at https://www.adb.org/terms-use#openaccess.

This CC license does not apply to non-ADB copyright materials in this publication. If the material is attributed to another source, please contact the copyright owner or publisher of that source for permission to reproduce it. ADB cannot be held liable for any claims that arise as a result of your use of the material.

Please contact pubsmarketing@adb.org if you have questions or comments with respect to content, or if you wish to obtain copyright permission for your intended use that does not fall within these terms, or for permission to use the ADB logo.

Corrigenda to ADB publications may be found at http://www.adb.org/publications/corrigenda.

Notes:
In this publication, "$" refers to United States dollars.
All photos by ADB unless stated otherwise.

Cover design by Jan Carlo Dela Cruz.

CONTENTS

TABLES AND BOXES

ACKNOWLEDGMENTS

Preparation of this *Build Back Better Sector Guides* series was led by Belinda Hewitt, senior disaster risk management specialist, Climate Change and Sustainable Development Department (CCSD), ADB with substantive inputs and review from Brigitte Balthasar, senior disaster and climate risk financing specialist, CCSD, ADB; Charlotte Benson, former principal disaster risk management Specialist, ADB; Alexandra Galperin, unit head, disaster risk management, CCSD, ADB; Steven Goldfinch, senior disaster risk management specialist, CCSD, ADB; Anne Orquiza, senior disaster risk management officer, CCSD, ADB; Grendel Saldevar, senior operations assistant, CCSD, ADB; and Mario Unterwaining, former disaster risk management specialist (resilient infrastructure), ADB. The series was developed in close collaboration with ADB Sectors Group and country teams. Margie Peters-Fawcett copy edited the volumes with the assistance of Cherry Lynn Zafaralla as proofreader. Layout was created by Rommel Marilla, page proofs checking by Levi Rodolfo Lusterio, and administrative support by Michelle Imperial.

This volume was authored by Belinda Hewitt with written inputs from Pawan Karki, former transport specialist, South Asia Regional Department, ADB. Case study inputs, review, and contributions to workshops were provided by Alexandra Pamela Chiang, senior advisor to the Vice President of Administration and Corporate Services (former transport specialist), ADB; Pinta Lizti Irene, associate project officer (infrastructure), Sectors Group (SG), Susan Lim, principal portfolio management specialist, Southeast Asia Regional Department (SERD), ADB; Amr J. Qari, country operations head, SERD, ADB; Eric Quincieu, principal water resources specialist, SG. Technical review by Rachael Jonassen with Amir Gilani and Tsutomu Nifuku of Miyamoto International is greatly appreciated.

ABBREVIATIONS

ADB   Asian Development Bank

BBB   build back better

DMC   developing member country

EAL   Emergency Assistance Loan

ITS   intelligent transport system

O&M   operation and maintenance

PDNA   post-disaster needs assessment

ADB Pakistan: National Disaster Risk Management Fund (50316–001). Aerial view of the Flood Emergency Reconstruction and Resilience Project in Jhelum River on Tuesday, 29 May 2018. The project is part of the National Disaster Risk Management Fund and aims to provide safety to the people of Jhelum City and the surrounding localities and villages from the floods.

Typhoon Ketsana (Ondoy) dropped 455 millimeters (17.9 inches) of rain on Metro Manila in a span of 24 hours on 26 September 2009. A month's worth of rainfall in a single day washed away homes and flooded large areas, stranding thousands in the city and nearby provinces and causing numerous fatalities.

I

INTRODUCTION

Timely support for recovery and reconstruction efforts is critical when a disaster occurs to minimize any potential long-term setbacks to sustainable and inclusive socioeconomic development. It is essential to provide a window of opportunity to rebuild assets and improve livelihoods to increase climate and disaster resilience and reduce the risk of future hazards. With impacts of disasters projected to rise in the coming decades as affected by climate change, unplanned urbanization, poor risk governance, and a range of other trends, challenges relating to climate uncertainty, growing complexity of infrastructure systems, and the compounding nature of multiple hazard events underline the importance of ensuring that communities and infrastructure systems are equipped to cope, adapt, and recover when faced with future shocks and stresses.

Developing member countries (DMCs) of the Asian Development Bank (ADB) bear a disproportionate share of impacts from geophysical and extreme weather hazard events. Between 2004 and 2023, these DMCs accounted for 55% of global disaster fatalities and 74% of people affected.[1] Over this 20-year period, ADB has provided more than $9.1 billion in financing for emergency assistance loan (EAL) projects relating to disasters triggered by natural hazards, conflict, displacement, food insecurity, and health emergencies. The support that ADB offers its DMCs aims at ensuring resilient post-disaster recovery, as well as strengthening long-term disaster risk reduction.

ADB's Strategy 2030[2] and 2021 Disaster and Emergency Assistance Policy[3] outline commitments to ensure effective response and support to build back better (BBB) after a disaster or emergency.[4] "Build back better" refers to the use of the early recovery and reconstruction phases after a disaster or emergency to increase resilience of nations and communities to future events by integrating risk reduction

---

1   Centre for Research on the Epidemiology of Disasters, EM-DAT: The International Disaster Database. www.emdat.be (accessed 5 February 2024). People affected by multiple disasters have been counted multiple times.

2   ADB. 2017. *Strategy 2030: Achieving a Prosperous, Inclusive, Resilient, and Sustainable Asia and the Pacific.*

3   ADB. 2021. *Revised Disaster and Emergency Assistance Policy.*

4   Strategy 2030 sets out a commitment to "provide assistance for disaster response, including support to build back better."

measures into the restoration of physical infrastructure, societal systems, livelihoods, economies, and the environment.[5] By systematically promoting risk-informed, well-designed, and timely recovery and reconstruction, ADB supports the implementation of international agreements, such as the Sendai Framework for Disaster Risk Reduction 2015–2030 and the 2030 Agenda for Sustainable Development Goals, including its 17 Sustainable Development Goals, both of which promote a comprehensive approach toward disaster risk management and BBB frameworks, including through community-based applications.

The six volumes that comprise the *Build Back Better Sector Guides* series aim to support ADB staff, consultants, and DMC counterparts to enhance the climate and disaster resilience of DMC communities, infrastructure, and systems through effective and well-designed post-disaster assistance. The volumes are based on principles, measures, and lessons learned from the international BBB literature; a review of over 40 ADB EALs processed between 2004 and 2021; and the outcome of consultations with a wide range of ADB staff.

Each of the volumes has been co-developed with relevant ADB sector and thematic groups. The sectors are areas in which ADB has played a key role in post-disaster recovery and reconstruction and where majority of ADB's disaster and emergency assistance has focused in the last 20 years. They are as follows:

(i)   Volume 1: Overview
(ii)   Volume 2: Transport
(iii)   Volume 3: Water, Sanitation, and Hygiene (WASH)
(iv)   Volume 4: Irrigated Agriculture
(v)   Volume 5: Social Infrastructure
(vi)   Volume 6: Power

This Volume 2: Transport provides an overview of good practice solutions, considerations, and lessons learned for building back better in the transport sector but does not represent a general or step-by-step handbook on methods to prepare and implement post-disaster needs assessment (PDNA) or EALs; nor does it for other forms of post-disaster assistance. The scope of this volume is limited to BBB considerations for surface transport (roads, railways and bridges) and has limited focus on other forms of transport infrastructure such as ports and airports.

The scope of this series includes building resilience in response to disasters triggered by natural hazards; however, some of its content is relevant to the broader aspect of economic recovery, including within the context of health emergencies and conflict. Complementary objectives, including equity and inclusion, green recovery, poverty reduction, and broader sustainable development are also presented.

---

[5]   Adapted from United Nations General Assembly. 2016. Report of the Open-Ended Intergovernmental Expert Working Group on Indicators and Terminology Relating to DRR. Seventy-First Session, Item 19(c).

ADB's Role in Resilient Post-Disaster Recovery and Reconstruction

Following a disaster, ADB can mobilize rapid post-disaster technical support under the second window of its Asia Pacific Disaster Response Fund in areas such as the preparation of PDNAs; government-led recovery plans; and post-disaster projects, including EALs. The PDNA is a well-established tailored methodology that is used for analyzing damage, loss, and needs prioritization. While the exercise should be led by the government, it is often conducted with the support of one or more international partners. The PDNA compiles information relating to the physical impacts of a disaster, economic value of damages and losses, human and macroeconomic impacts, and cost of early and long-term recovery needs and priorities. As such, the PDNA is an important tool to inform implementation of BBB through post-disaster programming.

Once recovery and reconstruction requirements have been assessed, ADB can mobilize finance for recovery and reconstruction through EAL, additional financing for pre-established projects, and investment projects that support longer-term reconstruction needs. ADB's 2021 Emergency Assistance Loan Policy enables the rapid approval of loans (within 12 weeks) to assist in the rebuilding of high-priority physical assets and the restoration of economic, social, and governance activities following disasters triggered by natural hazards, health emergencies, food insecurity, technological and industrial accidents, and post-conflict situations.[6] The Emergency Assistance Loan Policy and Disaster and Emergency Assistance Policy aim to support DMC's BBB efforts to enhance climate and disaster resilience. Table 1 provides a list of additional resources relating to ADB's policies and directives relating to post-disaster assistance.

Table 1: Key Documents on ADB Policies and Guidance for Post-Disaster Assistance

Document	Web Page
2021 Disaster and Emergency Assistance Policy	http:// www.adb.org/documents/revised-disaster-and-emergency-assistance-policy
Revised Emergency Assistance Loan Policy	http:// www.adb.org/documents/revised-emergency-assistance-loan-policy
Establishment of a Second Window of Assistance under the Asia Pacific Disaster Response Fund	http:// www.adb.org/documents/establishment-second-window-assistance-under-asia-pacific-disaster-response-fund
Post-Disaster Needs Assessment Guidelines	http:// www.recoveryplatform.org/pdna
Disaster Recovery Planning: Explanatory Note and Case Study	https://www.adb.org/publications/disaster-recovery-planning-explanatory-note-case-study

Source: Asian Development Bank.

---

6   ADB. 2021. *Revised Emergency Assistance Loan Policy*. Manila.

Importance of Long-Term Resilience Building

Long-term and upstream approaches to resilience building are critical to minimize the impacts of disasters and ensure more effective and efficient use of post-disaster assistance resources. ADB can play a key role in leveraging increased risk awareness to ensure resilience-focused upstream planning. Where risk-responsive socioeconomic development and sector plans are already in place ahead of a disaster, they can more effectively guide long-term disaster recovery and bring about a shift toward resilience and sustainable development.

Risk-informed sector plans enable more rapid and effective post-disaster recovery and reconstruction where they are informed by comprehensive multihazard disaster risk assessments and incorporate ex ante recovery planning. Past ADB EALs, such as the 2015 Nepal: Earthquake Emergency Assistance Project (see Volume 5: Social Infrastructure) and the 2018 Tonga: Cyclone Gita Recovery Project (see Volume 6: Power), aligned recovery planning with climate and disaster resilience objectives set out in existing sector programs, government road maps, and the national development plan.

Use of the Build Back Better Sector Guides

This sector guide is intended to be read in conjunction with the introductory "Build Back Better Sector Guide Volume 1: Overview." The overview guide covers the broad measures that are likely relevant to any post-disaster recovery and reconstruction project, regardless of sector.

While the volume does not provide detailed technical guidance, it does provide various additional technical resources that can guide project-specific decision-making (Appendix: Suggested Readings). For any given project, it is important that resilience measures are selected appropriately and on a project-by-project basis, informed by an understanding of the components of the transport infrastructure project and local context. There should be analysis of current and future risk; economic development objectives; economic feasibility and viability; as well as relevant policies, including climate and disaster risk management and safeguards requirements.

ADB Pakistan: National Flood Emergency Response (44356-022). Children play on a railway damaged by the Pakistan floods of September 2010. The ADB project rehabilitated roads and bridges damaged in the same event to higher levels of resilience and incorporated nature-based solutions.

Impacts of the 2004 Asian Tsunami on the coastline of Banda Aceh, Indonesia.

II
DISASTER IMPACTS AND RECOVERY OBJECTIVES

Natural hazard events in Asia and the Pacific have caused severe and widespread impact on transport systems, with transport damage and loss comprising a significant share of overall infrastructure sector recovery needs (Table 2). Physical damage to and disruption of transportation compounds disaster losses by hindering recovery efforts, limiting community access to basic needs and livelihoods, and interrupting supply chains.[7] Planning and building transport systems based on comprehensive climate and disaster risk assessment is critical to facilitate response and recovery efforts (e.g., evacuation, delivery of relief, and reinstatement of other critical infrastructure and services), and will allow for the continuation of economic activity. Reconstruction of transport infrastructure can provide an essential source of employment, which in turn will contribute to economic recovery, particularly when making use of locally sourced materials and services.

---

[7] Economic modeling suggests that indirect losses resulting from transport infrastructure failure represent a large share of the total cost of disasters. See E.E. Koks et al. 2019. A Global Multi-Hazard Risk Analysis of Road and Railway Infrastructure Assets. *Nature Communications*. 10 (Article 2677).

Table 2: Examples of Transport Sector Disaster Effects and Recovery Needs

Event	Disaster Effects (Damages and Loss) ($ million)		Recovery Needs ($ million)	
	Infrastructure[a]	Transport	Infrastructure[a]	Transport
Cyclone Pam (Vanuatu), 2015[b]	86	47 (55%)	57	36 (63%)
Earthquake (Nepal), 2015[c]	652	216 (33%)	743	282 (38%)
Landslides and Floods (Sri Lanka), 2017[d]	103	87 (84%)	170	100 (59%)
Floods (Lao People's Democratic Republic), 2018[e]	219	205 (87%)[f]	290	277 (85%)[f]

[a] Infrastructure damages and losses are defined based on the post-disaster needs assessment guidelines produced by the Global Fund for Disaster Reconstruction and Recovery (GFDRR. 2013. *Post-Disaster Needs Assessments: Guidelines—Volume A: Guidelines*). These guidelines include the water and sanitation, community infrastructure, energy, transport, and telecommunications sectors.
[b] Government of Vanuatu. 2015. Vanuatu Post-Disaster Needs Assessment: Tropical Cyclone Pam.
[c] Government of Nepal. 2015. *Nepal Earthquake 2015: Post Disaster Needs Assessment—Volume A: Key Findings*. National Planning Commission.
[d] Government of Sri Lanka. 2017. Sri Lanka Rapid Post Disaster Needs Assessment: Floods and Landslides. Ministry of National Policies and Economic Affairs and Ministry of Disaster Management.
[e] Government of Lao People's Democratic Republic. 2018. *Post-Disaster Needs Assessment 2018 Floods, Lao PDR*.
[f] Includes waterways.

Note: This table provides a selection of examples where transport sector disaster effects comprised a significant proportion of recovery needs following various natural hazard events. In instances where the required value is not available, the local currency was converted to United States dollars based on the exchange rate at the time of the event, and sourced from the World Bank's Development Indicators (accessed 1 June 2023).

Source: Asian Development Bank.

Between 2005 and 2021, transport infrastructure comprised over 30% of ADB's disaster and emergency assistance financing[8] relating to disasters triggered by natural hazards. A review of the projects shows that recovery and reconstruction efforts provide an opportunity to BBB by enhancing resilience, economic connectivity, and social and environmental outcomes. The challenge for ADB staff and DMCs, however, is the trade-off between the time it takes to plan, design, and construct better systems, and the rapid reinstatement of assets, given that transport is vital for the recovery of other sectors. The 2018 Indonesia: Emergency Assistance for Rehabilitation and Reconstruction project—Subcomponent 2 (Palu Bay Port Master Plan, 52316-001), for example, overcame these challenges by leveraging rapid technical assistance to develop a plan for sustainable and resilient recovery. In addition, innovative products such as prefabricated transport infrastructure elements can in some cases be adopted to achieve more timely and resilient recovery.

---

[8] Estimated at $1.93 billion, based on a review of disaster and emergency assistance projects approved for the period 2005–2018.

To a great extent, transport assets are exposed to natural hazards due to their wide spatial distribution and common setting along coastlines or on river floodplains. Eight of ADB's DMCs are ranked among the top 10 in a global study of absolute expected annual damage per kilometer of road and railway transport infrastructure (also footnote 19).[9] Developing countries in the Pacific region suffer from some of the worst expected annual damage relative to transport infrastructure value (also footnote 17).[10] Investing in more resilient transport infrastructure in high-risk locations often has a low incremental cost and is cost-effective in the long run, particularly in the case of new or reconstructed (rather than retrofitted) assets. This is in part attributed to future reductions in operation and maintenance (O&M) costs for assets constructed at higher levels of resilience. For effective resilience investment, however, it is important to have available adequate data, risk models, and decision-making methods.[11] Post-disaster recovery offers the opportunity to enhance overall resilience of asset networks, services, and users through risk-informed siting and alignment; improving diversity of routes and services; protection of critical assets; and assurance of adequate systems and resources for O&M and repair.

Global transport systems are evolving rapidly, due to transport mode shift and new technology favoring more efficient, smart, low-carbon, and high-occupancy solutions. Many of ADB's DMCs lack quality transport infrastructure and services, exacerbated by traffic congestion, transport pollution, and road fatalities—all of which pose major constraints to sustainable economic development. Beyond the core objectives to strengthen climate and disaster resilience, there is a need to reinstate transport systems in such a way as to close existing gaps in services and promote equity, be affordable and efficient, limit greenhouse gas emissions, and promote the use of renewable resources, as illustrated in Box 1.[12] Integrating these objectives into fast-tracked emergency projects will require upstream support for resilient transport planning, guidelines, and standards.

---

[9]   The People's Republic of China, Fiji, Indonesia, Papua New Guinea, the Philippines, and Viet Nam appear in ADB's top 10 ranked in terms of most severe multihazard risk (tropical cyclones [in terms of wind speed]), earthquakes, surface flooding, river flooding, and coastal flooding), with expected annual road and rail asset damage in United States dollars relative to each kilometer of transport infrastructure. Expected annual damage is based on direct damages and does not include transport delay and disruption costs nor wider economic impact.

[10] Four Pacific Island nations—Fiji, Papua New Guinea, Solomon Islands, and Vanuatu—are among the top 11 countries globally based on multihazard expected annual damage of road and rail assets relative to the country's infrastructure value.

[11] S. Hallegatte, J. Rentschler, and J. Rozenberg. 2019. *Lifelines: The Resilient Infrastructure Opportunity*. World Bank.

[12] ADB. 2022. *Reimagining the Future of Transport Across Asia and the Pacific*.

Box 1: Key Objectives for Post-Disaster Transport Recovery and Reconstruction

Resilient post-disaster recovery in the transport sector should reduce future damage and loss, as well as improve the resilience of transport assets, users, owners, and operators. Global best practices and lessons learned from Asian Development Bank (ADB) projects suggest that other key objectives should include the following:

- **Improve connectivity and reliability** to enable long-term economic recovery and revitalization, with future growth and transport needs in mind.
- **Improve transport accessibility and equity,** particularly for women and girls, poor people, those with disabilities, older adults, and other marginalized populations.
- **Enhance transport safety** and address the chronic socioeconomic burden of road trauma through design, road user education, and capacity building.
- **Leapfrog to green, efficient, smart, and low-carbon solutions** that promote decarbonization and demotorization of the transport sector, in support of Nationally Determined Contributions and healthy environments.

Further useful information is provided in *Reimagining the Future of Transport across Asia and the Pacific.*[a]

---

[a] ADB. 2022. Reimagining the Future of Transport Across Asia and the Pacific.

Source: Asian Development Bank.

ADB Vanuatu: Cyclone Pam Road Reconstruction Project (49319-001). The project supported the reconstruction of the transport sector infrastructure on Efate ring road damaged by the Cyclone Pam floods and storm surges in March 2015.

ADB Maldives: Tsunami Emergency Assistance Project (39099-013). The dock in a community of Dhidhdhdoo Island after the 2004 tsunami. The project rehabilitated the harbor, incorporating a range of resilient materials.

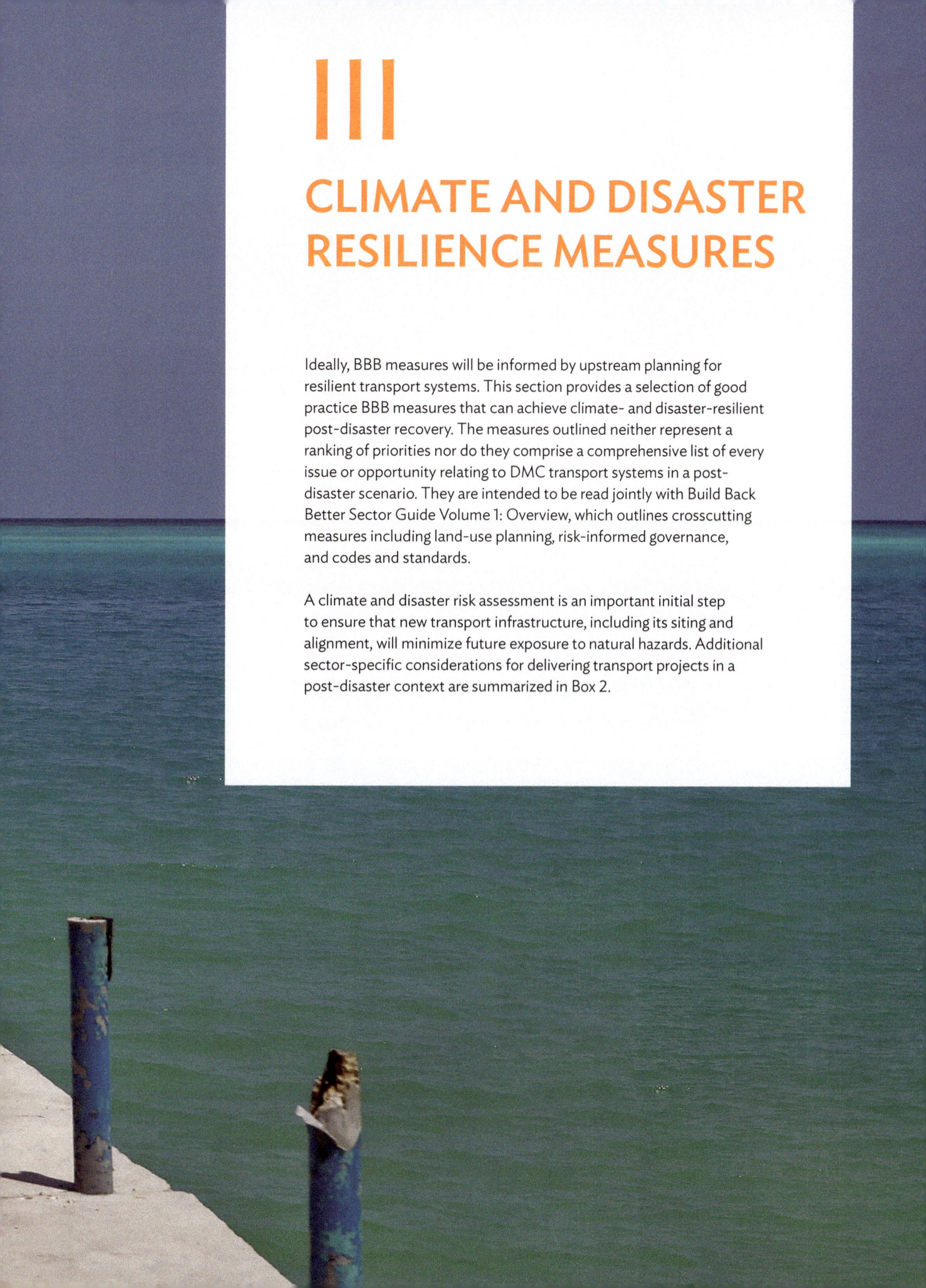

III

CLIMATE AND DISASTER RESILIENCE MEASURES

Ideally, BBB measures will be informed by upstream planning for resilient transport systems. This section provides a selection of good practice BBB measures that can achieve climate- and disaster-resilient post-disaster recovery. The measures outlined neither represent a ranking of priorities nor do they comprise a comprehensive list of every issue or opportunity relating to DMC transport systems in a post-disaster scenario. They are intended to be read jointly with Build Back Better Sector Guide Volume 1: Overview, which outlines crosscutting measures including land-use planning, risk-informed governance, and codes and standards.

A climate and disaster risk assessment is an important initial step to ensure that new transport infrastructure, including its siting and alignment, will minimize future exposure to natural hazards. Additional sector-specific considerations for delivering transport projects in a post-disaster context are summarized in Box 2.

Box 2: Considerations for Delivering Transport Projects in a Post-Disaster Context

To deliver transport programming in a post-disaster context, it is necessary to consider particular constraints, challenges, and opportunities, such as the following:

- **Time pressure.** While many post-disaster assistance projects are under significant time constraints, transport projects particularly are, given the need for the speedy delivery of relief, reparation of assets, and economic recovery. The emergency assistance completion reports and regional case studies of the Asian Development Bank indicate that time constraints can contribute to an acceleration of capital works with poor cross-sector coordination and quality control, inadequate design reviews (particularly of complex structures such as bridges), lack of construction oversight, and deficient road subsurface preparation. In some cases, these have led to structural integrity and safety issues, resulting in greater economic loss in the long term, additional requirements for replacement or repair, and network disruptions and downtime. Where possible, therefore, short-term solutions such as temporary routes and services should be created so that there is sufficient time for the design and delivery of a lasting and resilient transport system.
- **Knock-on impacts of decision-making.** Following severe damage or heightened risk levels (e.g., slope failure or destabilization), decisions on whether to reinstate, realign, or decommission transport infrastructure as part of a transport recovery plan have significant impact on people, existing infrastructure, and regional connectivity, particularly in the case of a managed retreat. A decision to realign or not reinstate transport infrastructure may restrict access to local communities and livelihoods. Decisions will require careful consideration of technical and economic feasibilities (e.g., whole-of-lifecycle costs); social and economic implications (e.g., future emergency access/exit facilities); and stakeholder consultation. Where resilience-focused transport plans are already in place ahead of a disaster, this can inform more effective reconstruction decision making.
- **Labor and material needs.** Transport projects, particularly in the case of road restoration, require significant volumes of construction materials and labor, compared to other sectors. Failure to prioritize transport sector restoration may lead to shortages and drive up the cost of reconstruction for other sectors and stakeholders, including housing. While use of local materials is recommended, material shortages may be a challenge and the environmental impact of large-scale resource extraction must be carefully considered. Use of recycled materials (including building rubble, waste polymers, and unused excavated material) should be explored for construction alongside conventional materials.

Source: Asian Development Bank.

Network Planning, Integration, and Redundancy

Reconstruction on a wide scale presents an opportunity to review the performance of transport systems and existing bottlenecks from the local to national levels, so that network improvements will enhance performance in future emergencies. Improving network redundancy and diversity can ensure that if one route or service is affected by a disaster, alternative routes and modes can be used for safe evacuation, delivery of essential goods and services and relief, and access for repair, as illustrated in Nepal and Samoa (Box 3).

> ### Box 3: Project Examples—Network Integration and Redundancy
>
> The eastern and western regions of Nepal were isolated following the devastating floods of 2008. The **Nepal: Emergency Flood Damage Rehabilitation Project**[a] (43001-012) of the Asian Development Bank (ADB) was instrumental in construction of a permanent bridge over the Koshi River at Chatara, deemed strategically essential to ensure passageway of the East–West Highway year-round. Construction included an alternative route for safe movement of people and goods between the eastern and western parts of Nepal in case of future flooding.
>
> In Samoa, the Cross Island Road provides a critical alternative between the island's northern and southern coasts in the event of cyclone and tsunami warnings for evacuation. As a result of the devastating impacts of Tropical Cyclone Evan in 2012, a significant portion of the road network fell into disrepair and became unsafe, particularly in the hilly areas. ADB's **Samoa: Central Cross Island Road Upgrading Project**[b] (51268-001) strengthened the climate and disaster resilience of Samoa's coastal communities by upgrading 20 kilometers of the main road link for future safe evacuation. Despite not being delivered during the recovery phase, the project nevertheless ultimately responded to the long-term recovery needs that were identified following the cyclone. The project also addressed climate-responsive road maintenance and the capacities of Samoa's Land Transport Authority.
>
> [a] ADB. Nepal: Emergency Flood Damage Rehabilitation Project.
> [b] ADB. Samoa: Central Cross Island Road Upgrading Project.
>
> Source: Asian Development Bank.

Transport modes should be integrated so that in normal as well as disaster conditions, people are able to move safely and in a timely way, relief supplies can be delivered effectively, and repair services can be delivered. For example, in coastal areas of Bangladesh, improved integration of inland water transportation services (ferries) with land transport modes such as roads and railways has generated joint benefits for the economy and enabled evacuation ahead of coastal hazard events.

A priority consideration for post-disaster transport planning is whether to relocate or realign transport infrastructure to reduce hazard exposure and future disaster impacts. Such decisions require careful consideration of social and economic factors. With regard to linear transport, challenges include steep slopes (grades of 60%–70% and above); deep-seated rotational landslides; and sections prone to shallow landslides, torrents, avalanche chutes, rock-falls, wet areas, saturated soils, and highly erodible soils.

Green Transport Networks

Repair and reconstruction of transport corridors provides an opportunity to prioritize water management and nature-based solutions as part of planning and design for some components of the transport network. In the case of wide transport corridors, regreening strategies can generate catchment level benefits including reducing disaster risk, enhancing water and air quality, and generating biodiversity.

On a site-specific level, reconstruction of linear assets should be planned and delivered in a manner that considers form and function within the local landscape and water catchment. This is essential to not only prevent the impact of new risks (e.g., increased flooding because of blocked natural flow paths) but also to leverage potential beneficial roles such as use of roads as flood barriers.

Areas prone to high flooding, landslides, or erosion can be protected by green transport solutions that can help improve surface water management by controlling the speed of runoff, capturing surface flows, stabilizing soils, and influencing the sedimentation process in catchments. An integrated approach to green transport network planning can provide opportunities to generate further benefits, such as roads in arid areas designed to harvest water so that surface flow is redirected for recharging, storage, and application to agricultural land.[13] An example of green transport networks as part of BBB is provided in Box 4.

Box 4: Green Transport Networks: Project Example

The **Pakistan: Flood Emergency Reconstruction and Resilience Project** (49038-001) of the Asian Development Bank supported the rehabilitation and reconstruction of high-priority infrastructure, including roads and bridges following the 2014 flooding and landslides in Pakistan's northern regions. Nature-based solutions and bioengineering were employed as a slope stabilization technique to reduce future landslide risk. Planting of road corridors provided a vital post-disaster income opportunity to community members, including a large proportion of women.

Source: ADB. Pakistan: Flood Emergency Reconstruction and Resilience Project.

Intelligent Transport Systems

An intelligent transport system (ITS) collects and shares real-time data on user traffic, environmental conditions, asset conditions, and network performance in an effort to accurately predict future traffic demand and incremental risk and to enable adaptive management, operation, and maintenance.[14] ITS can be integrated with early warning systems (EWS) to allow transport operators and users to detect hazards and respond in real time (e.g., rerouting services or initiating emergency operating protocols). ITS can also provide a broader range of benefits, such as artificial intelligence and machine learning, to support real-time traffic optimization. ITS is also used to inform the travel public of forecast risks and advise them of ways to avoid hazards.

---

[13]   F. van Steenbergen et al. 2021. *Green Roads for Water: Guidelines for Road Infrastructure in Support of Water Management and Climate Resilience*. World Bank.

[14]   Examples of intelligent transport systems in relation to hazards or emergencies include (i) Hazus Program (Federal Emergency Management Agency of the US Department of Homeland Security; and (ii) Safety Intelligent Disaster Decision Support System (The University of Melbourne's Centre for Disaster Management and Public Safety).

Post-disaster recovery activities have shown that ITS is cost-effective when combined with reconstructed or new infrastructure in lieu of retrofitting. Smart solutions do not necessarily require the roll-out of extensive high-tech applications; rather, they can be simple and economical (e.g., incorporating sensors for flood or landslide detection and geographic information systems for improved network planning and management). Implementing ITS in a manner that is viable and sustainable in the long run requires clear definition of local maintenance and repair needs, adequate skills and resources, and simple back-up systems in the event of systems failure. It is important to ensure key stakeholder engagement to raise the understanding and management capacities necessary for ITS platforms. Two different examples of ITS are provided in Box 5.

Box 5: Intelligent Transport Systems Project Examples

Although Intelligent Transport Systems (ITS) have yet to be adopted in the context of emergency assistance by the Asian Development Bank (ADB) their use is becoming increasingly widespread in the Asian and Pacific region. For example, ADB's **Uzbekistan: Central Asia Regional Economic Cooperation Corridor 2 Karakalpakstan Road (A380 Kungrad to Daut-Ata Section) Project** (48414-006)[a] includes ITS to provide real-time information on road conditions (including climate hazards) to transport authorities and drivers.

In Singapore, drones are used to inspect rail track and tunnel conditions, whereas in Indonesia, the government has implemented ITS to enhance Jakarta's road user information and traffic control systems. In Japan, seismometers have been installed along railway tracks, which are able to capture ground motion and trigger the deceleration of trains in the event of an earthquake.

[a] ADB. Uzbekistan: Central Asia Regional Economic Cooperation Corridor 2 Karakalpakstan Road (A380 Kungrad to Daut-Ata Section) Project.

Source: ADB.

Resilient Structures

Asset vulnerability can be minimized by designing and constructing more resilient transport infrastructure and by providing protective infrastructure. Structural measures to achieve higher levels of climate and disaster resilience are specific to transport asset type, location, and hazard profile. Selection of structural resilience measures must be based on an understanding of class of transport infrastructure components, climate change scenarios, vulnerability to identified hazards, and projected impacts over the infrastructure lifetime. Measures should account for both physical and operational performance.

Resilience to climate change refers not only to the robustness and flexibility to adapt or modify infrastructure and transport system operation over time in response to climate change, but also to changing user requirements. "Designing in" flexibility for future upgrades (e.g., modular wharf structures that can be adapted in response to future sea level rise) can be a suitable alternative where the cost of fully implementing climate proofing measures cannot be justified.

Some broad resilience considerations for specific infrastructure types are outlined below:

(i) **Terminals and stations**. High occupancy assets should be located and designed with particular attention to minimizing exposure to hazards, enhancing structural integrity, ensuring emergency access and egress, and allowing for safe failure and predictable damage control on the pre-designed elements. Suitable contingency systems should be provided, such as back-up power supply, pumping systems, and evacuation routes with adequate signage. Where stations and terminals can provide shelter during future emergencies, this may warrant use of higher design safety factors that can withstand more extreme conditions (e.g., higher wind speed or ground acceleration and an enhanced performance objective).

(ii) **Roads and railways.** Alignment should be improved to minimize exposure to hazards (including unstable slopes). Camber, horizontal, and vertical profiles also should be more efficient to avoid water pooling issues and safety. Designs should consider emergency access and egress routes, including adequate access for emergency vehicles, maintenance and repair equipment, and community evacuation. Refuge areas (e.g., hard shoulders and roadside platforms) should be provided at key locations, including approaches to large bridges, areas with high flood risk, and emergency vehicle sites. In flood-prone locations, nature-based and structural measures for flood protection are important. In areas that extreme heat can be a hazard, use of innovative pavement material and rail can be considered.

(iii) **Bridges.** Climate and disaster risk should be reduced through risk-informed siting and elevation, and appropriate design measures should be adopted to address key risks (e.g., enhanced piles, bearings, and abutments). There should be adequate protection for scour and erosion. Sufficient capacity for future heavier truck load and traffic loads (including heightened loads for emergency and evacuation scenarios) should be provided to enhance the safety of all users—including separate tracks for pedestrians and cyclists, where possible. Inspection and testing prior to commissioning should be ensured. A regular and periodic inspection program should be implemented and preventative maintenance measures documented during the inspections to be programmed.

(iv) **Wharves**. There should be appropriate elevation or landward siting of decks, wharf aprons, and critical structures, as well as provision of protective infrastructure (including structural solutions such as sea walls or nature-based solutions) to help reduce the risk of disasters and accommodate climate change impacts, including sea level rise and changes in wave climate. Safety of life during future disasters can be enhanced through strategic siting of high occupancy buildings, and by ensuring safe evacuation routes are provided.

Achieving a resilient transport infrastructure network requires enhancing the continuity and reliability of critical supporting infrastructure and services, in particular, ensuring resilient power system arrangements for transportation signaling systems and essential rail services. Risk of power supply disruption due to disaster impacts may be reduced by enhancing cabling and line arrangements, providing surge protection, ensuring critical energy assets are in safe and elevated locations, and putting in place controls to allow rapid shut down of connections.

Improved outcomes for transportation resilience, safety, and accessibility can be enabled through a user-centered design approach that includes consultation with transport users and communities to understand their requirements and behavior (including when disasters and other forms of disruption occur) as part of transport recovery planning processes. This should include consideration of differential needs of various vulnerable groups, such as women, people with limited mobility, and poor people. A user-centric approach can help to ensure that transport infrastructure and services are more comfortable, safe, and accessible for all users. Although this is challenging in the post-disaster context, key opportunities include integrating strong sector consultation in PDNA preparation and including resources and terms of reference for consultation and outreach as part of project implementation. Examples of ADB BBB support for more resilient transport structures in the PRC and Solomon Islands are shown in Box 6.

Box 6: Project Examples—Resilient Structures

The **Solomon Islands: Emergency Assistance Project** (41105-012)[a] of the Asian Development Bank (ADB) supported the rehabilitation and maintenance of roads, bridges, footbridges, wharf, and jetty that were damaged and destroyed by an 8.1 magnitude earthquake. Australian and New Zealand design standards were adopted as the most appropriate in lieu of local standards to reduce further vulnerability to natural hazards. Bridges and beams were anchored to pile abutments to prevent the rising of bridge decks from their supports. Road drainage was reinforced with concrete culverts, replacing existing structures.

The **China, People's Republic of: Emergency Assistance for Wenchuan Earthquake Reconstruction Project** (42496-013)[b] provided support to the government for the reconstruction and rehabilitation of damaged roads and bridges in two provinces following the destruction caused by a magnitude 8 earthquake that struck southwest of the country in 2008. Geologic and hazard assessments immediately following the earthquake informed infrastructure design. Disaster resilience was achieved by adopting higher standards based on revised seismic codes. Roads were paved in a way to ensure rural residents had all-weather access to markets, schools, clinics, and other facilities, while civil works provided geotechnical protection.

[a] ADB. Solomon Islands: Emergency Assistance Project.
[b] ADB. China, People's Republic of: Emergency Assistance for Wenchuan Earthquake Reconstruction Project.

Source: Asian Development Bank.

Resilient Materials Selection

Construction materials to strengthen climate and disaster resilience are specific in terms of transport asset type, and depend highly on the location, design, and type of hazard (Box 7). For post-disaster reconstruction, materials must be selected with care, bearing in mind functional requirements (e.g., performance, availability and familiarity of the contractors for use of such material, local conditions, hazards, maintenance implications) and availability, as well as sustainability and cost. Evaluating which materials functioned well or failed based on learning from previous disaster and climate impacts can help to inform context-specific resilience solutions. The selection of materials should be undertaken as early as possible in post-disaster recovery, as it has important implications for road thickness and pavement design. Regardless of selection of material, certification showing compliance with referenced standards should be required prior to use in construction. Further, as part of construction quality management, samples should be taken and tested to confirm such compliance.

It is potentially more economical to select materials that are robust, durable, and self-maintaining when rebuilding in remote and high-risk locations and/or for low-use infrastructure. Railway tracks, for instance, may select slab rather than ballasted track and bitumenous over conventional granular sub-ballast layers; or, in relation to roads, double bituminous surface treatments or concrete pavement may be preferable. Where hazards occur frequently and infrastructure is relatively accessible, however, it may be more cost effective to adopt a "patch and repair" approach, by combining suitable yet economical materials and simple construction techniques with risk-informed operation and maintenance regimes. This latter approach should be informed by transport network risk assessment, combined with comprehensive arrangements for asset monitoring, emergency response and repair activities, and coordinated as part of an asset management program that addresses repairs in a timely manner. Economic appraisal will be necessary to determine the most viable and cost-effective approach. Examples of context-specific selection of resilient materials are shown in Box 7.

Box 7: Project Examples—Selection of Resilient Materials

The **Cambodia: Flood Damage Emergency Reconstruction Project**[a] (46009-001) of the Asian Development Bank, for which additional financing was approved in 2013, supported the reconstruction of roads and bridges damaged and destroyed by the Mekong River floods of 2011 and flashfloods of 2013. Road sections were built with higher quality materials than the previous laterite stone paving, including double bituminous surfacing and/or concrete paving. These new materials should prolong the lifecycle of the roads and bridges as well as improve resistance to future flooding.

The **Maldives: Tsunami Emergency Assistance Project**[b] (39099-013) was instrumental in the reconstruction of several islands devastated by the 2004 India earthquake and tsunami. The reconstruction and upgrade of Dhidhdhoo Island Harbor in the capital of Maldives incorporated a range of resilient materials. These included an enduring rock type for the seawalls in contrast to the previous gunny sacks with cement, which decompose within a few years; steel piling for the quay; and reinforced concrete for the docking areas.

[a]   ADB. Cambodia: Flood Damage Emergency Reconstruction Project.
[b]   ADB. Maldives: Tsunami Emergency Assistance Project.

Source: Asian Development Bank.

Enhanced Drainage

Where water-related hazards are a challenge for transport infrastructure and, particularly, where building back follows damage due to extreme precipitation or flooding, it important to provide adequate water drainage and retention systems to account for future rainfall and flood scenarios based on assessment of future climate scenarios. Improper alignment and inadequate drainage are among the most common causes of transport infrastructure failure when natural hazard events occur, particularly for surface roads. Wherever possible, low-impact and nature-based drainage and retention solutions should be adopted; these can include swales, permeable pavement, vegetation, and wetland restoration methods, all of which are able to contribute to co-benefits such as the reduction of air and water pollution from vehicular traffic and the effects of urban heat islands, as well as improved ecology.

Transport corridors have the potential to interrupt catchment drainage and perpetuate flooding and waterlogging in local communities, particularly those designed above grade. Care is also required when installing additional drainage infrastructure, such as culverts or water bars, to ensure that these neither increase future erosion nor affect wildlife. However, if well-designed, transport corridors can provide a first line of flood defense for communities and productive land, and wildlife crossings and fish passages can be incorporated to address biodiversity concerns. To achieve such benefits, it is important to ensure drainage design is informed by catchment-level hydrological assessment, with a broader view of post-disaster reconstruction and future land use.

Slope Stabilization and Erosion Control

Post-disaster, it is essential to establish the reasons for slope instability based on a detailed geotechnical evaluation and slope stability analysis to identify other potential landslide areas. Unstable slopes and erosion could be the result of heavy rainfall and surface runoff during storms, seepage of water under the surface causing slip failure or slip-circle, absence of base rock, presence of thick and soft overburden that flows once saturated, base rock movement or slips, man-made disturbances such as toe excavation, or toe cutting by river flows.

Where risk assessment and geotechnical studies identify a need, or where slope failure or erosion has already contributed to infrastructure failure or damage, relocate or realign infrastructure to reduce future hazard exposure when practical. In many cases, however, it is impossible to relocate the infrastructure or fully eliminate the risks, thus calling for slope stabilization and erosion control measures. An economic appraisal of transport route reconstruction should factor in the cost of slope protection and stabilization, O&M in the long term, and the economic impact of potential downtime when future slope failure occurs.

There are numerous solutions to prevent future slope destabilization and erosion. These include surface drainage management, bioengineering, toe protection, masonry, concrete or gabion retaining walls, anchoring systems, crib walls, and knitted geotextiles. Bioengineering is a subset of green infrastructure that utilizes vegetation to serve an engineering function, such as soil surface protection against erosion, soil stabilization, and improved drainage functions. Bioengineering techniques often provide a highly cost-effective method of surface protection for soil slopes by using vegetation to armor the surface against erosion, such as through direct seeding, brush layers and fascines (bundles of live woody stems), or truncheon cuttings. As with other types of nature-based solutions, bioengineering can provide significant co-benefits in the form of enhancing biodiversity, improving air and water quality, and ensuring gender-inclusive livelihood opportunities, among others, in the event of a disaster.

Adequate scour and erosion protection is of particular importance in areas where the daylight point of pipe and culvert outlets is located over a soil slope, as well as for bridge piers and abutments located in streams and waterways. Ideally, slope stabilization measures should be implemented in combination with adequate monitoring and management—including for landslides and scour where relevant. Two examples of comprehensive approaches to slope stabilization as part of BBB in Bangladesh and Cambodia are provided in Box 8.

Box 8: Project Examples—Enhanced Drainage, Slope Stabilization, and Erosion Control

The 2005 **Bangladesh: Emergency Flood Damage Rehabilitation Project** (38625-013) of the Asian Development Bank (ADB) provided support for the rehabilitation and resumption of railways and services between flood-affected areas. Geotextile technology was applied for slope protection on railway embankments, reducing not only the need for temporary repair work but also savings in government expenditures over the long term. Municipal roads were resealed and repairs were carried out on the potholes, eroded sub-base, bridges, and drains or culverts of 55 *pourashavas* (secondary level towns). This resulted in significant improvement to drainage units and the living conditions of town residents.

The 2011 **Cambodia: Flood Damage Emergency Reconstruction Project** (46009-001) received additional financing in 2013, which supported the reconstruction of damaged and/or destroyed roads and bridges as a result of the 2011 Mekong River floods and 2013 flashfloods. The project was able to improve the resilience of roads and bridges to flooding by providing slope stabilization. Gabion retaining structures were built near major bridges and road embankments close to the Mekong River, and side drains were created in urban areas. Grass planting improved the stability of slopes along roads. New drainage systems enhanced the capacity to accommodate increased flood risk due to climate change. A network of hydromet and automatic weather stations was created to support flood early warning. The project also sought to ensure long-term commitment and funding for adequate road maintenance.

Source: ADB. Bangladesh: Emergency Flood Damage Rehabilitation Project; and ADB. Cambodia: Flood Damage Emergency Reconstruction Project.

Transport Sector Capacity Development

Many ADB emergency assistance projects in the transport sector include institutional and technical capacity building for road and other transport authorities, such as in the PRC, to implement resilient O&M practices and better respond to future disasters (Box 9). These include support to enhance budgeting; network risk assessment; risk monitoring; contingency and evacuation planning (including disaster response and recovery planning for ministries, local authorities, and transport operators); and risk-informed infrastructure design and O&M. For further information on capacity building, see Volume 1.

Box 9: Project Example—Transport Sector Capacity Building

In 2009, the **China, People's Republic of: Emergency Assistance for Wenchuan Earthquake Reconstruction Project** (42496-013) of the Asian Development Bank provided capacity building to executing and implementing agencies on adopting recent updates to seismic engineering standards and codes, risk-informed operation and maintenance practices; and management, technical, and administrative capacities in the construction and maintenance of rural roads, bridges, and schools. Experience gained from the project has benefited other government-financed projects.

Source: ADB. China, People's Republic of: Emergency Assistance for Wenchuan Earthquake Reconstruction Project.

The lack of adequate resources, skills, and planning for regular, periodic, and preventative maintenance are recognized as key factors that contribute to the vulnerability of transport infrastructure to climate and disaster impacts, particularly for linear assets. For example, failure to seal and repair cracks and potholes in road surfaces in a timely manner leads to seepage of surface water and weakening of pavement sublayers. Priority areas for improving the resilience of transport asset management include ensuring regular and timely maintenance and repair of infrastructure, debris clearing for culverts and bridge channels, and vegetation clearing. Maintenance and repair needs are likely to change and increase in many DMCs due to increased frequency and severity of extreme weather events due to climate change.

Box 10: Case Study—Port Master Plan for Palu Bay, Indonesia

Located in the Makassar Strait between the islands of Borneo and Sulawesi in Indonesia, Palu Bay is an important regional hub for Indonesia's sea transportation. On 28 September 2018, a series of strong earthquakes in the neck of the Minahasa Peninsula triggered underwater landslides and local tsunamis around the bay. Among the devastating impacts to the local population and the widespread damage, the ports in the bay were severely hit, causing a drastic decline in capacity and performance.

Initial support for disaster response and recovery from the Asian Development Bank (ADB) included an emergency grant[a] from the Asia Pacific Disaster Response Fund (October 2018) and a quick-disbursing loan for Emergency Assistance for Recovery and Rehabilitation from Recent Disasters[b] (November 2018), along with various other technical assistance grants for post-disaster needs assessments, preparation of engineering designs, and support for the recovery Master Plan. As part of the recovery planning process, ADB assisted Indonesia's Ministry of National Development Planning to produce a disaster-prone zone draft based on ground surveys, stakeholder consultation, and risk assessments. The findings were incorporated into the recovery plan to inform reconstruction and thus reduce exposure of the area to future hazard events.

continued on next page

Box 10 *continued*

In 2019, ADB approved the Emergency Assistance for Rehabilitation and Reconstruction Project[c] Component 2: Transportation Infrastructure, focusing on the recovery of Indonesia's main port of Pantoloan in Palu Bay, as well as those of Donggala and Wani, among other activities. The project documents clearly identified lessons from past ADB post-disaster reconstruction projects and objectives for building back better. These included designing disaster-resilient infrastructure based on international good practices, new technology, alternative construction materials, and the importance of strengthening the capacity of national agencies on constructing disaster- and climate-resilient infrastructure.

PRE-EARTHQUAKE

POST-EARTHQUAKE

Source: Map data Google Earth ©2018 Centre national d'études spatiales and Airbus.

Pantoloan Port. Aerial views, pre- and post-earthquake (photo by the Indonesia Directorate General of Sea Transportation).

The project's initial priority was to develop master plans of the ports to guide effective economic development and BBB. During the early stages of work, the design team undertook a review of the changes to land-use planning (the draft disaster-prone zone) and the design standards that were implemented following the earthquake and identified site-level implications. For example, the site of Pantoloan was rezoned as "Forbidden Zone 4," representing a tsunami-prone area. In response to lower density land-use requirements associated with the zoning, the port storage, road, and office areas were reconfigured, with office buildings relocated further southeast from the shoreline. Peak ground acceleration projections also were revised to significantly higher levels. In addition, cost estimates for new port structures were revised to include increased seismic design standards.

Development of the master plans included regional development analyses and predictions of future demands based on economic and population growth. Project objectives (beyond build back better) were a sustainable "green port," reduction of environmental impacts, with gender responsive and inclusive features. ADB also intends to reinforce the capacity building of port operations and of safety and emergency response plans.

[a] ADB. Indonesia: Sulawesi Tsunami Emergency Response.
[b] ADB. Indonesia: Emergency Assistance for Recovery and Rehabilitation from Recent Disasters.
[c] ADB. Indonesia: Emergency Assistance for Rehabilitation and Reconstruction.

Source: Asian Development Bank.

Landslide in Nepal during road construction.

SUGGESTED READINGS

The following technical and subject matter resources are further references in implementing nonstructural build back better measures.

ADB. 2024. Green Roads Toolkit.

ADB. 2011. Guidelines for Climate Proofing Investment in the Transport Sector, Road Infrastructure Projects.

ADB. 2020. Bioengineering for Green Infrastructure.

ADB. 2020. *Manual on Climate Change Adjustments for Detailed Engineering Design of Roads Using Examples from Viet Nam.*

Argyroudis et al. 2019. Fragility of Transport Assets Exposed to Multiple Hazards: State-of-the-Art Review Toward Infrastructural Resilience. *Reliability Engineering & System Safety.* 191. 106567.

GFDRR. 2018. Transport Sector Recovery: Opportunities to Build Resilience. Global Fund for Disaster Reconstruction and Recovery.

Jovanovski et al. 2019. Build Back Better Approach to Recovery of Flood-Damaged Transport and Water Infrastructure. Conference Paper. September.

D. Marcelo, S. House, and A. Raina. 2019. Incorporating Resilience in Infrastructure Prioritization - Application to the Road Transport Sector, Policy Research. *Working Paper.* No. 8584. World Bank.

Markolf et al. 2019. Transportation Resilience to Climate Change and Extreme Weather Events: Beyond Risk and Robustness. *Transport Policy. 74.* pp. 174–186.

T. Maynard, T. 2017. Future Cities: Building Transport Infrastructure Resilience. *Emerging Risk Report 2017, Society and Security.* Lloyd's.

Resilience Shift. 2019. Various Industry Guides to Enhancing Resilience: Rail, Roads, Ports.

Steenberg et al. 2021. Green Roads for Water: Guidelines for Road Infrastructure in Support of Water Management and Climate Resilience. World Bank.

UITP. 2016. Urban Rail, Climate Change and Resilience. International Public Transport Union.

S. Weilant, A. Strong, and B.M. Miller. 2015. Incorporating Resilience into Transportation Planning and Assessment. Rand Corp.

World Bank, 2017. Climate and Disaster Resilient Transport in Small Island Developing States: A Call for Action.

www.ingramcontent.com/pod-product-compliance
Lightning Source LLC
LaVergne TN
LVHW071457180726
843512LV00018B/1406